FUELING THE FUTURE
Solar Energy

Chris Oxlade

Heinemann Library
Chicago, Illinois

Customer Service 888–454–2279
Visit our website at www.heinemannraintree.com

Photo research by Rebecca Sodergren and Hannah Taylor
Designed by Richard Parker and Q2A Solutions
Illustrations by Jeff Edwards
Originated by Chroma Graphics (Overseas) Pte Ltd
Printed and bound in China by Leo Paper Group

12 11 10 09 08
10 9 8 7 6 5 4 3 2 1

Library of Congress Cataloging-in-Publication Data
Oxlade, Chris.
  Solar energy / Chris Oxlade.
      p. cm. -- (Fueling the future)
  Includes bibliographical references and index.
  ISBN 978-1-4329-1564-3 (hc) -- ISBN 978-1-4329-1570-4 (pb) 1. Solar energy--Juvenile literature. I. Title.
TJ810.3.O95 2008
  333.792'3--dc22
                              2007050767

Acknowledgments

The author and publisher are grateful to the following for permission to reproduce copyright material:
©Alamy pp. 18 (i love images), 23 (Jim West); ©Corbis pp. 12 (Nick Rains), 13 (Beateworks/David Burton), 4
Corbis Royalty Free; ©GeorgiaTech p. 26; ©Getty Images pp. 22 (Dennis Doyle), 24 (Gallo Images); ©NASA
p. 27; ©PA Photos p. 9 (AP); ©Science Photo Library pp. 5, 14 (Martin Bond), 6 (NASA), 10 (Peter Menzel),
11 (Maximillian Stock Ltd), 15 (NASA/Dryden Flight Research Center Photo Collection), 16 (John Mead), 25
(Eurelios/Patrick Dumas); ©SolucarEnergia p. 17; ©Still Pictures pp. 7 (Mark Edwards), 21 (Jorgen Schytte).

Cover photograph of solar power generators, White Cliffs, NSW, reproduced with permission of
©Photolibrary.com/Robin Smith. Cover background image of blue virtual whirl reproduced with permission of
©istockphoto.com/Andreas Guskos.

The publishers would like to thank David Hood of the Centre for Alternative Technology for his help in the
preparation of this work.

Every effort has been made to contact copyright holders of any material reproduced in this book. Any
omissions will be rectified in subsequent printings if notice is given to the publisher.

Disclaimer

Contents

Some words are shown in bold, **like this**. You can find out what
they mean by looking in the glossary.

Why Do We Need Energy?

Energy makes everything in the universe happen. It makes plants grow, it makes lights glow, and it makes you walk and talk. The energy we discuss in this book is the energy that we use as we go about our lives. We need energy for transportation, to keep warm or cool, to cook food, to operate machines, to light buildings and streets, and to produce things in factories.

Every light in this city needs energy from somewhere to make it glow.

Where does our energy come from?

All the energy we use comes from energy sources. The most common sources are coal, oil, and natural gas, which are known as **fossil fuels**. They are used to **generate electricity** and as fuels for heating and transportation. Electricity is also generated at **nuclear power** stations. We also generate electricity from flowing water (a form of energy called **hydroelectricity**), wind, **tides** and waves, and from the sun—these are known as **renewable** energy sources, because they will never run out.

Solar energy is energy from the sun. Solar cells like these turn solar energy into electricity.

The need for renewables

Most scientists agree that our use of fossil fuels is causing serious environmental problems. The worst of these is **global warming**, which in turn is causing **climate change**. Fossil fuels will also run out eventually. This is why we need to be less dependent on fossil fuels and use more energy from renewable sources, such as the sun.

The energy we use

We use a staggering amount of energy. Every second, all of us in the developed world use up enough energy to keep a lightbulb lit for nearly half a million years. As the world's population grows, we will need more and more energy.

What Is Solar Energy?

"Solar **energy**" is the name given to any energy we get from the sun. But where does this energy come from? There are **nuclear reactions** happening in the center of the sun all the time. These reactions give out huge amounts of energy. The energy moves out to the surface of the sun. It is given out into space in the form of **radiation**. The two main types of radiation are light and heat. Heat is also known as **infrared** radiation. Solar energy is a **renewable** form of energy because the sun will keep shining (and so give out energy) for billions of years.

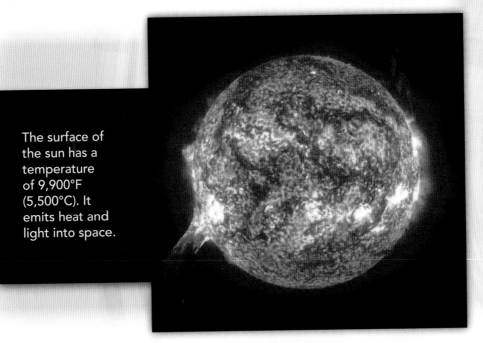

The surface of the sun has a temperature of 9,900°F (5,500°C). It emits heat and light into space.

How does the sun's energy reach Earth?

Heat and light from the sun travel as rays, in straight lines. They spread out through space in all directions from the sun, moving at the speed of light, which is 186,000 miles (300,000 kilometers) per second. A tiny fraction of the rays hit Earth, which is 93 million miles (150 million kilometers) away. Some of the heat and light that hits Earth bounces off the **atmosphere** and back into space. Just over half reaches the surface, where we can collect it and put it to use.

This large mirrored dish is a solar cooker. It concentrates heat energy from the sun (called solar thermal energy) onto the pan in the center, where the heat cooks food. This cooker is being used in India, where it saves people from searching for firewood, and from breathing in smoke from a wood fire. There is more information about capturing heat energy from the sun on page 18.

Total solar energy

The sun gives out an incredible amount of energy, but nearly all of it misses Earth. Less than one-billionth arrives here. Even so, this is a huge amount of energy. Enough energy hits each square foot of the surface to operate a small appliance such as a hair dryer. In all, the solar energy that hits Earth is 10,000 times as much as we need.

Does the sun heat Earth?

Heat rays from the sun that hit Earth's surface make the surface warm. The heating effect is greatest at the equator, where the rays hit the surface straight on. In many parts of the world, the heating effect is also greater in summer than in winter, because the sun is higher in the sky then and the days are longer.

The warm surface of Earth heats the air above it. This heat makes the air swirl around, which creates the world's weather systems and causes wind and rain. So, the energy we get from the wind and from flowing water originally comes from the sun.

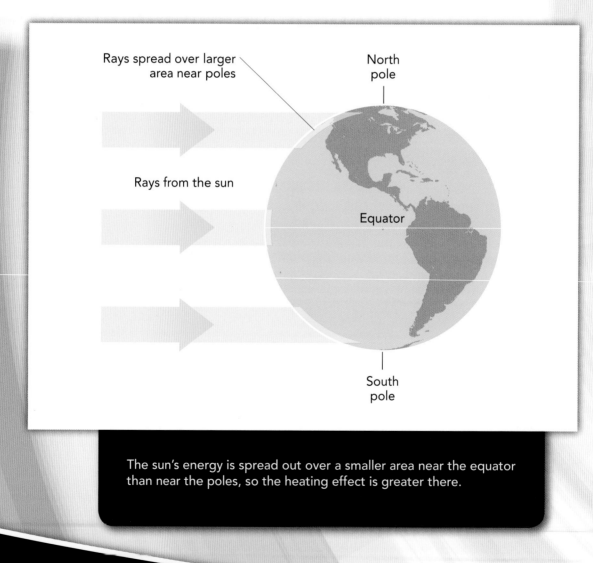

The sun's energy is spread out over a smaller area near the equator than near the poles, so the heating effect is greater there.

This flooding in the city of Villahermosa, Mexico, occurred in 2007.

What is the greenhouse effect?

Some of the heat that Earth's surface gives off gets trapped by gases in the atmosphere, instead of escaping into space. This is known as the **greenhouse effect**. This effect is becoming stronger because humans are adding a gas called carbon dioxide to the atmosphere by burning **fossil fuels**. Carbon dioxide helps to trap heat. This is known as **global warming**, and it is causing changes in the world's weather patterns. These changes are known as **climate change**.

Fossil fuels from the sun

Fossil fuels are made from the remains of animals and plants that lived thousands or millions of years ago. These animals and plants used energy from the sun to grow. So, the energy released when we burn them originally came from the sun. It has been trapped inside Earth for many years.

One way of capturing light from the sun is to turn it into **electricity**. We do this with a device called a **solar cell**. The scientific name for a solar cell is a **photovoltaic** cell or PV cell.

You can see the individual solar cells in this solar panel.

How do solar cells work?

A solar cell is made of a special type of material called a **semiconductor**. Two slightly different layers of semiconducting material are placed one on top of the other. Each layer is connected to a wire. When light hits the layers of semiconducting material, it frees tiny particles called **electrons**. When the solar cell is connected to an **electric circuit**, the electrons flow around the circuit, forming an electric **current**. The solar cell does the same job as a battery. It pushes electricity around a circuit when light hits it.

Solar cells are made on discs of semiconducting material.

How much electricity does a solar cell produce?

The brighter the light that hits a solar cell, the more electricity it produces. But even in bright sunlight, a single solar cell produces only a very tiny amount of electricity. So, solar cells are normally joined together to provide more electricity. Together, the solar cells are known as a solar panel or solar module. A solar panel the size of this book produces enough electricity to operate a medium-sized portable radio.

Improving technology

The solar cells we are using at the moment are not very **efficient**. The best (and most expensive) ones convert just one-fifth of the light that hits them into electricity. Cheaper solar cells convert just one-tenth of their light into electricity. However, new types of solar cell are being developed all the time, and in the future solar cells will become much cheaper and more efficient.

Solar cells have a wide range of uses, from powering electronic watches and calculators to producing **electricity** at solar **power** stations. Solar cells are becoming more popular as they become cheaper and we learn more about the environmental problems caused by burning **fossil fuels**.

Using solar cells eliminates the need to use electricity from other sources, such as household electricity supplies, which are made mainly by burning fossil fuels.

Solar cells are useful in remote areas where there is no electricity. Here they power a telephone booth.

Small-scale solar cells

Many small electronic devices, such as watches and calculators, need only a tiny amount of electricity to work. They can be powered by a small solar cell built into the case. These devices normally have batteries, too. When light falls on the solar cell, the electricity it produces makes the device work. In the dark, the batteries take over. The solar cells allow the batteries to last longer.

Can we use solar cells outside?

Solar cells work best outdoors, where there is plenty of light to turn into electricity. They are also useful in powering devices that are a long way from electrical outlets or power supplies. For example, a solar garden fountain uses solar cells to produce the electricity for its water pump. On a larger scale, solar cells power remote weather stations and electronic road signs.

Solar recharging

Small solar panels can be used to recharge the batteries in portable devices such as cell phones and laptop computers. The solar panel does the same job as a charger that plugs into an electrical outlet. In strong sunshine the solar panel can operate the device at the same time.

Solar cells for buildings

Solar cells are used on a large scale to provide electricity for homes, schools, and offices. At night, or when it is very cloudy, electricity is taken from the **electricity grid** instead. In remote areas, where there is no electricity grid, the electricity produced by solar cells during the day can be stored in rechargeable high-capacity batteries. The batteries provide electricity at night, when the solar cells are not working.

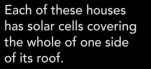

Each of these houses has solar cells covering the whole of one side of its roof.

Where are the solar cells in buildings?

The sun shines most on a building's roof and on the side of the building that faces the sun as the sun moves across the sky. (For example, in the northern hemisphere, this is the south side of the building.) These are where solar panels are placed to catch the most sunshine. Some new homes and offices are being built with solar cells built into the structure itself. Using solar cells like this is called building-integrated **photovoltaics** (BIPVs). Cells can now be built into roof tiles, wall panels, and even transparent glass windows. Solar cells are an important part of "zero-**emission**" or "zero-carbon" buildings. These are buildings that use **renewable** sources to produce all the electricity they need.

Helios is an unmanned, experimental solar-powered aircraft.

Can solar cells power vehicles?

Experimental lightweight solar-powered cars have been built and have been driven for hundreds of miles on solar power alone. However, solar-powered family cars are a long way off, as the electricity from the number of solar cells that can fit on a car body is not enough to power a standard car.

Back to the grid

During the day, when its solar panels are producing large amounts of electricity, a building can send any extra electricity into the electricity grid. The electricity company buys the extra electricity, so the building works like a mini power station. This is called grid tying.

Solar cells for power stations

Millions of individual solar cells combined together produce as much electricity as a small coal-fired power station. So, solar cells can be used to build electricity-**generating** stations that provide electricity for thousands of homes. These are called photovoltaic (PV) power stations.

A heliostat is a solar panel that tilts and swivels to follow the sun through the day.

How does a solar power station work?

A PV power station is made up of hundreds or thousands of solar panels, each made up of thousands of solar cells. For maximum power, the solar cells must face the sun straight on. Because the sun moves across the sky as day passes, the solar panels are often placed on swiveling mountings that follow the sun. **Transformers** change the electricity from the panels into a form that can be fed into the electricity grid.

This is one of the many new photovoltaic power stations in Spain.

Where are solar-cell power stations built?

PV power stations are only built in places where there are plenty of guaranteed sunny days. These places are normally toward the equator, where the sun gets high in the sky and shines strongly down, such as the southern United States and Africa. However, PV power stations have been built farther away from the equator, in places such as Germany and Holland.

Solar power in Spain

Spain is one of the hottest European countries with, on average, 340 sunny days every year. It is also a leader in solar **energy**. It is building both PV power stations and solar **thermal** power stations (see page 22). It plans to have 30 percent of its electricity generated by renewable resources by 2010, with a large proportion coming from solar energy. In Spain, government laws mean that all new buildings must have solar panels installed.

How Do We Capture Heat from the Sun?

Heat comes from the sun in the form of heat **radiation**, which is called **infrared** radiation. You can feel this heat on your face in the sunshine. This radiation also heats up the ground and objects left in the sun, such as cars. Things heat up in the sunshine because they soak up the heat rays. We can capture this heat and use it for heating. The heat captured can also be used to **generate electricity** (see page 22).

The warmth of the sun we enjoy on the beach can generate electricity for us.

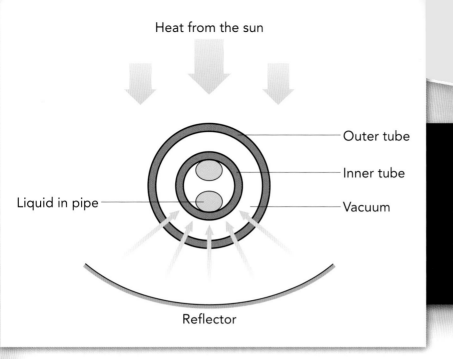

Heat from the sun

Outer tube

Inner tube

Vacuum

Liquid in pipe

Reflector

This diagram shows a cross section of part of a solar thermal collector. The reflector focuses heat onto the central tubes.

Solar thermal collectors

A device that collects heat **energy** from the sun is called a solar **thermal** collector. (The word "thermal" means "heat.") The main part of a solar thermal collector is a large panel that is placed in the sunshine. Inside the panel are pipes full of liquid. Heat from the sun is trapped by the panel and heats up the liquid. The most efficient design for a solar collector is called an evacuated tube collector. Its pipes are inside glass tubes that have the air pumped out of them. This stops the heat of the liquid from escaping back into the air. Shiny reflectors under the tubes concentrate heat onto them.

Black and white

Solar thermal collectors make use of a simple scientific principle: dark colors absorb (take in) heat rays, while light colors and mirrors reflect heat rays. Mirrors are used to reflect heat onto the pipes in a collector, and the pipes are painted black so that they absorb as much heat as possible.

The most common use of solar **thermal energy** is to heat water for washing and cleaning. Solar water heaters are installed in many houses, schools, offices, and hotels in places with sunny climates. Solar thermal energy is also used on a giant scale to **generate electricity** for **electricity grids**.

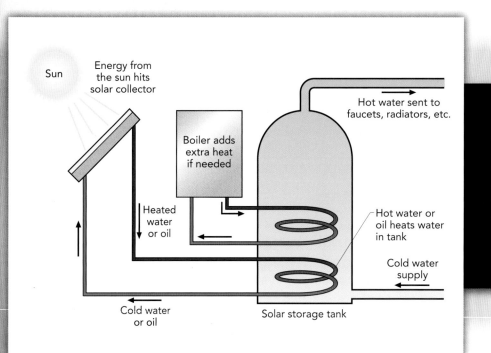

Sun

Energy from the sun hits solar collector

Boiler adds extra heat if needed

Hot water sent to faucets, radiators, etc.

Heated water or oil

Hot water or oil heats water in tank

Cold water supply

Cold water or oil

Solar storage tank

This diagram shows a heating and hot-water system that combines solar thermal collectors and a conventional boiler.

Heating water with solar energy

A solar water heating system is made up of a solar thermal collector and a storage tank. When the sun shines on the thermal collector, the water inside the panel's pipes is heated up. The heated water is pumped from the panel along a pipe to a hot-water tank. Cooler water from the tank flows to the panel to replace it. As the water circulates, it gets hotter and hotter. The solar energy saves electricity or gas that would normally be used for heating water. Even in countries with a cool climate, solar systems can provide half the energy used for water heating.

This house in India has solar water heaters on the roof. The tank holds the hot water.

Passive solar heating

You have probably noticed that rooms get warm when the sun shines through windows on summer days. Heat rays heat surfaces in the room, which in turn heat the air in the room. This effect is called passive solar heating, because it happens without the need for special equipment to capture the heat. We rely on passive solar heating to heat greenhouses and conservatories. Many modern buildings are designed to make use of passive solar heating in order to keep the space inside warm. They use shades to control the amount of heat that gets in. In fact, solar heat can be used to cool a building by letting the heat create drafts that draw in cool air.

What is a solar thermal power station?

Solar thermal energy is also used to generate electricity. At a solar thermal **power** station, heat is trapped by collectors and used to boil water to produce steam. The steam drives **turbines**, which in turn operate **generators** that produce electricity. This is exactly what happens in coal-fired power stations, except that now the heat comes from the sun instead of from burning fuel. It is different from a PV power station, where light is turned straight into electricity.

This power tower is at Sanlucar la Mayor, near Seville in Spain. Hundreds of mirrors concentrate the sun's heat onto the top of the tower. The energy produces electricity for 6,000 homes. This was the first commercial solar thermal station in the world.

Solar thermal power stations work like a magnifying glass, by concentrating the sun's heat into one spot.

Thermal collectors

At a solar thermal power station, heat is trapped by huge thermal collectors that produce much higher temperatures than the solar thermal collectors people have in their homes. There are two main designs of solar thermal power station.

In the first system, called a power tower, hundreds of huge mirrors reflect heat onto the top of a tower, where a special liquid gets heated. The heat is transferred to water to make it boil. The photo on page 22 shows a power tower.

In the second system, called a trough collector, there are long U-shaped troughs with mirrors on the inside. Oil-filled pipes run through the troughs. Heat is concentrated onto the pipes, heating the oil. The oil carries the heat to the generating area, where it boils water. The cooled oil returns to the troughs to be heated again. The photo on this page shows a trough collector.

Concentrating rays

The mirrors at a solar thermal power station are designed to catch as much heat as possible. At a power tower station, the mirrors work together like a giant dish-shaped mirror. They reflect heat rays so that the rays all meet at one place. The mirrors in trough collectors are specially shaped so that all the heat rays that enter the trough are reflected onto the pipe.

Solar **energy** is not perfect. Like any other form of energy, it has benefits (pros) and disadvantages (cons).

Solar energy is suitable in remote areas. This solar panel provides electricity for floating homes on Lake Titicaca in Bolivia.

The pros of solar energy

Solar energy is free because sunshine is free. However, it is only available after a solar energy system has been paid for. It is **emission**-free. This means that **solar cells** and panels do not produce polluting gases or carbon dioxide that lead to **global warming**. Solar energy is also a **renewable** form of energy. It will never run out, because the sun will keep shining for billions of years to come. Solar energy is an excellent source of energy in remote areas where there is no central supply of **electricity**. Also, electricity **generated** by solar cells in a building that is not being used can be fed back to the **electricity grid**. Finally, passive solar heating can keep a building warm without the need for any other form of heating.

Once installed, solar cells need almost no maintenance.

The cons of solar energy

The technology of solar cells poses several problems that still need to be solved. The solar cells we have today are not **efficient** at converting light to electricity. This means that very high numbers of solar cells are needed to produce a large amount of electricity. The solar cells are also expensive to make and buy. The high costs of building solar **power** plants means that electricity from them is currently three times as expensive as from other types of power station. Also, solar cells and solar **thermal** collectors do not produce energy when it is dark or very cloudy outside. So, solar energy is not efficient in places where the skies are often cloudy, or near Earth's poles, where the sun is normally low in the sky.

Payback time

At present, the equipment used to trap solar energy is expensive. The cost of installing a system is high. But then the savings from not using other forms of energy, such as natural gas, gradually pay for the system. Still, it can take many years to regain the money. The "payback" period is long.

What Is the Future of Solar Energy?

Currently, solar **energy** makes up just 1 percent of all the energy we use, but solar energy is here to stay. All the time, the technology of solar energy is improving, its costs are coming down, and the use of solar energy is spreading.

This is an experimental 3D solar cell, which contains microscopically small towers that capture light energy.

What is new in solar technology?

New types of **solar cells** are being developed. **Organic** solar cells are based on plastics, rather than traditional **semiconductors**, which are made from crystals of **silicon**. They are cheap and easily built into other materials. Multi-junction solar cells are made up of many thin layers and can capture more light energy than traditional cells. They may have efficiencies up to 40 percent, compared with less than 20 percent today.

This is an artist's impression of Sun Tower, a design for a solar satellite to send solar energy to Earth.

An important resource

Solar energy is one of the main **renewable** energies that we will rely on in the future. We need to develop the technology to make it more **efficient**. And we must keep building solar power stations so that our reliance on **fossil fuels** is reduced. If we covered one-thousandth of Earth's surface with solar cells, we could **generate** all the **electricity** we need. Perhaps one day we will. Solar energy is a technology that will help save the planet.

In the distant future

Two ideas for large-scale electricity production are the solar tower and solar satellite. In a solar tower, heat rays from the sun warm air in a giant glass-covered space. The hot air rushes up a tall chimney, powering **turbines** on the way. A solar tower with a chimney over half a mile (1 kilometer) high is planned for Australia. Solar satellites with huge solar panels would orbit Earth, collecting energy and sending it down to receivers on Earth by powerful microwaves. In orbit, they would collect sunlight 24 hours a day.

Solar Energy Timeline

212 BCE	Greek soldiers may have set fire to an enemy Roman ship by concentrating the sun's rays with their metal shields.
100 CE onward	Roman bathhouses use passive solar heating to keep the space inside warm.
1767	Horace de Saussure, a Swiss scientist, builds the first solar collector, which is used for cooking.
1839	In France, Edmond Becquerel discovers that light can produce an electric **current** when it hits certain materials. (This is called the photovoltaic effect.) The effect will later be used in **solar cells**.
1876	The first simple solar cell is made, from a material called selenium.
1891	The first solar water heater is patented.
1905	Albert Einstein explains the photoelectric effect.
1954	A team of scientists at Bell Laboratories in New Jersey makes the first practical solar cell, based on **silicon**.
1958	Satellites begin to use solar cells to power their **electric circuits**.
1969	The first experimental concentrating solar **power** station is built in France.
1970s	Due to improving technology, the cost of solar cells falls five times.
1978	A small **photovoltaic** power station is built in Arizona.
1981	*Solar Challenger*, a solar-powered aircraft, flies across the English Channel.
1982	An experimental solar power station, Solar One, begins operating in California.
1986	A large trough collector is built in California. It is still the world's largest solar power station.
1999	A skyscraper is built in New York that uses building-integrated photovoltaics (BIPVs) to provide some of its electricity.
2000	Solar panels are installed on the International Space Station.
2001	NASA's Helios solar-powered plane reaches an altitude of 96,800 feet (29,500 meters).
2006	Europe's largest solar **thermal** power station begins operating in southern Spain.
2007	The 0.6-mile- (1-kilometer-) high Solar Tower is planned in Australia.

Solar Energy Facts and Figures

- The **power** output of a power station is measured in watts (W), kilowatts (kW), or megawatts (MW). A watt is a measure of how much energy is produced or used every second. A standard lightbulb needs between 50 and 100 watts, and a home needs about 1 kW on average. An average coal-fired power station provides around 1,000 MW, enough for a million homes.

- A small battery-charging solar panel provides a few watts of power. That is enough power to work a portable radio.

- A typical rooftop solar panel with an area of about 10 square yards (8 square meters) provides 1 kW of power. That is enough to power about 8 televisions.

- The world's largest solar **thermal** power station is Kramer Junction in California. It provides 150 MW—enough for a large town—using trough collectors.

- In 2007 the world's largest **photovoltaic** power station was in Germany, producing 12 MW—enough for a small town.

- Portugal plans to build a 116 MW photovoltaic power station, which would easily be the world's largest, capable of powering 120,000 homes.

- In 2007 solar energy provided less than 1 percent of the world's energy needs. Solar thermal power provided most of that 1 percent, with photovoltaics providing just a tiny fraction.

- Experts estimate that we will get just 5 percent of our energy from solar sources by 2040, but the figure may rise to 70 percent by 2100.

Glossary

atmosphere layer of air gases that surround the Earth

climate change changes in the world's patterns of weather caused by global warming

current flow of electric charge around an electric circuit

efficient something that does not waste much energy

electric circuit loop of wire and other components around which electricity flows

electricity form of energy. Electricity normally comes in the form of electrons moving along a wire.

electricity grid system of cables and other machinery that carries electricity from power plants to places where the electricity is used

electron tiny particle that is part of an atom

emission any gases given off when a fuel is burned, such as water vapor and carbon dioxide

energy ability to do work

fossil fuel fuel formed millions of years ago from decayed animals and plants

generate produce—for example, to produce electricity

generator machine that produces electricity when its shaft is spun around

global warming gradual increase in the temperature of Earth's land and water

greenhouse effect way that heat from the sun is trapped in Earth's atmosphere by certain gases in the air

hydroelectricity electricity produced from the energy in flowing water

infrared heat that travels in rays at the speed of light

nuclear to do with the nuclei (central part) of atoms

nuclear reaction change in the nucleus of an atom when particles leave the nucleus, the nucleus splits up, or particles are added to it

organic made from natural materials—for example, plant or animal materials

photovoltaic (PV) material that produces electricity from light. Solar cells are made from photovoltaic material.

power measure of how fast energy is produced or used up. It is measured in watts.

radiation energy in the form of rays, such as light and infrared

renewable able to be replaced over time

semiconductor material that can work as a conductor (allowing electricity to flow through it), but also as an insulator (resisting the flow of electricity)

silicon chemical used to make many types of electronic components, such as photovoltaic cells

solar cell device that produces electricity when light falls on it

thermal to do with heat

tide rise and fall in the sea level at coasts

transformer electric device that changes the voltage of electricity

turbine device with fans that spin when gas or liquid flows through it. In power stations they allow steam or water to turn electricity generators.

Find Out More

Books

Binns, Tristan Boyer. *A Bright Idea: Conserving Energy*. Chicago: Heinemann Library, 2005.

Oxlade, Chris. *Global Warming*. Mankato, Minn.: Capstone, 2003.

Royston, Angela. *The Day the Sun Went Out: The Sun's Energy*. Chicago: Raintree, 2006.

Websites

California's Solar Energy Program
www.gosolarcalifornia.ca.gov

Center for Renewable Energy and Sustainable Technology
www.crest.org

Solar Energy International
www.solarenergy.org/resources/youngkids.html

U.S. Department of Energy
www1.eere.energy.gov/solar

Index